CAN WE BE GOOD
WITHOUT GOD?

CAN WE BE GOOD WITHOUT GOD?

On the Political Meaning of Christianity

G LENN T INDER

REGENT COLLEGE PUBLISHING
Vancouver, British Columbia

This edition published 2007 by
Regent College Publishing
5800 University Boulevard, Vancouver, BC V6T 2E4 Canada
www.regentpublishing.com

Views expressed in works published by Regent College Publishing
are those of the author and do not necessarily represent the official
position of Regent College <www.regent-college.edu>.

"Can we be good without God?" was first published in the
December 1989 issue of *The Atlantic Monthly*.

A cataloguing record for this publication is available from
Library and Archives Canada

ISBN-10: 1-57383-042-9
ISBN-13: 978-1-57383-042-3

CONTENTS

INTRODUCTION

We are so used to thinking of spirituality as withdrawal from the world and human affairs that it is hard to think of it as political. Spirituality is personal and private, we assume, while politics is public. But such a dichotomy drastically diminishes spirituality, construing it as a relationship to God without implications for one's relationship to the surrounding world. The God of Christian faith (I shall focus on Christianity, although the God of the New Testament is also the God of the Old Testament) created the world and is deeply engaged in the affairs of the world. The notion that we can be related to God and not to the world — that we can practice a spirituality that is not political — is in conflict with the Christian understanding of God.

And if spirituality is properly political, the converse also is true, however distant it may be from prevailing assumptions: politics is properly spiritual. The spirituality of politics was affirmed by Plato at the very beginnings of Western political philosophy and was a commonplace of medieval political thought. Only in modern times has it come to be taken for granted that politics is entirely secular. The inevitable result is the demoralization of politics. Politics loses its moral structure and purpose, and turns into an affair of group interest and personal ambition. Government comes to the aid of only the well organized and influential, and it is limited only where it is checked by countervailing forces. Politics ceases to be understood as a pre-eminently human activity and is left to those who find it profitable, pleasurable, or in some other way useful to themselves. Political action thus comes to be carried out purely for the sake of power and privilege.

It will be my purpose in this essay to try to connect the severed realms of the spiritual and the political. In view of the fervent secularism of many Americans today, some will assume this to be the opening salvo of a fundamentalist attack on "pluralism." Ironically, as I will argue, many of the undoubted virtues of pluralism — respect for the individual and a belief in the essential equality of all human beings, to cite just two — have strong roots in the union of the spiritual and the political achieved in the vision of Christianity. The question that secularists have to answer is whether these values can survive without these particular roots. In short, can we be good without God? Can we affirm the dignity and equality of individual persons — values we ordinarily regard as secular — without giving them transcendental backing? Today these values are honored more in the breach than in the observance; Manhattan Island alone, with its extremes of sybaritic wealth on the one hand and Calcuttan poverty on the other, is testimony to how little equality really counts for in contemporary America. To renew these indispensable values, I shall argue, we must rediscover their primal spiritual grounds.

Many will disagree with my argument, and I cannot pretend there are no respectable reasons for doing so. Some may disagree, however, because of misunderstandings. A few words at the outset may help to prevent this. First, although I dwell on Christianity, I do not mean thus to slight Judaism or its contribution to Western values. It is arguable that every major value affirmed in Christianity originated with the ancient Hebrews. Jewish sensitivities on this matter are understandable. Christians sometimes speak as though unaware of the elemental facts that Jesus was a Jew, that he died before even the earliest parts of the New Testament were written, and that his scriptural matrix was not Paul's Letter to the Romans or the Gospel of John but the Old Testament. Christianity diverged from Judaism in answering one question: Who was Jesus? For Christians, he was the anticipated Messiah, whereas for the traditional Jews (Paul and the first Christians were of course also Jews), he was not. This divergence has given Christianity its own distinctive character, even though it remains in a sense a Jewish faith.

The most adamant opposition to my argument is likely to come from protagonists of secular reason — a cause represented pre-eminently by the Enlightenment. Locke and Jefferson, it will be asserted, not Jesus and Paul, created our moral universe. Here I cannot be as disarming as I hope I was in the paragraph above, for underlying my argument is the conviction that Enlightenment rationalism is not nearly so constructive as is often supposed. Granted, it has sometimes played a constructive role. It has translated certain Christian values into secular terms and, in an age becoming increasingly secular, has given them political force. It is doubtful, however, that it could have created those values or that it can provide them with adequate metaphysical foundations. Hence if Christianity declines and dies in coming decades, our moral universe and also the relatively humane political universe that it supports will be in peril. But I recognize that if secular rationalism is far more dependent on Christianity than its protagonists realize, the converse also is in some sense true. The Enlightenment carried into action political ideals that Christians, in contravention of their own basic faith, often shamefully neglected or denied. Further, when I acknowledge that there are respectable grounds for disagreeing with my argument, I had secular rationalism particularly in mind. The foundations of political decency are an issue I wish to raise, not settle.

1

CHRISTIAN LOVE

Love seems as distant as spirituality from politics, yet any discussion of the political meaning of Christianity must begin by considering (or at least making assumptions about) love. Love is for Christians the highest standard of human relationships, and therefore governs those relationships that make up politics. Not that political relationships are expected to exhibit pure love. But their place in the whole structure of human relationships can be understood only by using the measure that love provides.

The Christian concept of love requires attention not only because it underlies Christian political ideas but also because it is unique. Love as Christians understand it is distinctly different from what most people think of as love. In order to dramatize the Christian faith in an incarnate and crucified God, Paul spoke ironically of "the folly of what we preach," and it may be said that Christian love is as foolish as Christian faith. Marking its uniqueness, Christian love has a distinctive name, agape, which sets it apart from other kinds of love, such as philia, or friendship, and eros, or erotic passion.

When John wrote that "God so loved the world, that he gave his only Son," he illuminated the sacrificial character of divine love. This is the mark of agape. It is entirely selfless. If one could love others without judging them, asking anything of them, or thinking of one's own needs, one would meet the Christian standard. Obviously, no one can. Many of us can meet the requirements of friendship or erotic love, but agape is beyond us all. It is not a love toward which we are naturally inclined or for which we have natural capacities. Yet it is not something exclusively divine, like omnipotence, which human beings would be presumptuous to emulate. In fact, it is demanded of us. Agape is the core of Christian morality. Moreover, as we shall see, it is a source of political standards that are widely accepted and even widely if imperfectly, realized.

The nature of agape stands out sharply against the background of ordinary social existence. The life of every society is a harsh process of mutual appraisal. People are ceaselessly judged and ranked, and they in turn ceaselessly judge and rank others. This is partly a necessity of social and political order; no groups whatever — clubs, corporations, universities, or nations — can survive without allocating responsibilities and powers with a degree of realism. It is partly also a struggle for self-esteem; we judge ourselves for the most part as others judge us. Hence outer and inner pressures alike impel us to enter the struggle.

The process is harsh because all of us are vulnerable. All of us manifest deficiencies of natural endowment — of intelligence, temperament, appearance, and so forth. And all personal lives reveal moral deficiencies as well — blamable failures in the past, and vanity, greed, and other such qualities in the present. The process is harsh also because it is unjust. Not only are those who are judged always imperfect and vulnerable, but the judges are imperfect too. They are always fallible and often cruel. Thus few are rated exactly, or even approximately, as they deserve.

There is no judgment so final nor rank so high that one can finally attain security. Many are ranked high; they are regarded as able, or wise, or courageous. But such appraisals are never unanimous or stable. A few reach summits of power and honor where it seems for a moment that their victory is definitive. It transpires, however, that they are more fully exposed to judgment than anyone else, and often they have to endure torrents of derision.

Agape means refusing to take part in this process. It lifts the one who is loved above the level of reality on which a human being can be equated with a set of observable characteristics. The agape of God, according to Christian faith, does this with redemptive power; God "crucifies" the observable, and always deficient, individual, and "raises up" that individual to new life. The agape of human beings bestows new life in turn by accepting the work of God.

The power of agape extends in two directions. Not only is the one who is loved exalted but so is the one who loves. To lift someone else above the process of mutual scrutiny is to stand above that process oneself. To act on the faith that every human being is a beneficiary of the honor that only God can bestow is to place oneself in a position to receive that honor. (That is not the aim, of course; if it were, agape would be a way of serving oneself and would thus be nullified.) Agape raises all those touched by it into the community brought by Christ, the Kingdom of God. Everyone is glorified. No one is judged and no one judges.

Here we come to the major premise (in the logic of faith, if not invariably in the history of Western political philosophy) of all Christian social and political thinking — the concept of the exalted individual. Arising from agape, this concept more authoritatively than any other shapes not only Christian perceptions of social reality but also Christian delineations of political goals.

2

THE EXALTED INDIVIDUAL

To grasp fully the idea of the exalted individual is not easy, but this is not because it rests on a technical or complex theory. The difficulty of grasping the concept is due to its being beyond the whole realm of theory. It refers to something intrinsically mysterious, a reality that one cannot see by having someone else point to it or describe it. It is often spoken of, but the words we use — "the dignity of the individual," "the infinite value of a human being," and so forth — have become banal and no longer evoke the mystery that called them forth. Hence we must try to understand what such phrases mean. In what way, from a Christian standpoint, are individuals exalted? In trying to answer this question, the concept of destiny may provide some help.

In the act of creation God grants a human being glory, or participation in the goodness of all that has been created. The glory of a human being, however, is not like that of a star or a mountain. It is not objectively established but must be freely affirmed by the one to whom it belongs. In this sense the glory of a human being is placed in the future. It is not a mere possibility, however, nor does it seem quite sufficient to say that it is a moral norm. It is a fundamental imperative, even though all of us, in our sinfulness, to some degree refuse it. This fusion of human freedom and divine necessity may be summarily characterized by saying that the glory of an individual, rather than being immediately given, is destined.

Destiny is not the same as fate. The word refers not to anything terrible or even to anything inevitable, in the usual sense of the word, but to the temporal and free unfoldment of a person's essential being. A destiny is a spiritual drama.

A destiny is never completely fulfilled in time, in the Christian vision, but leads onto the plane of eternity. It must be worked out in time, however, and everything that happens to a person in time enters into eternal selfhood and is there given meaning and justification. My destiny is what has often been referred to as my soul.

Realizing a destiny is not a matter of acquiescing in some form of relentless causality. If it were, there would be no sin. A destiny can be failed or refused. That is why it is not a fate. True, the very word "destiny" is indicative of necessity, but the necessity of a destiny is not like the necessity that makes an object fall when it is dropped. Rather, it is the kind I recognize when I face a duty I am tempted to evade and say to myself, "This I must do." Yet my destiny has a weight unlike that of any particular duty, since it is the life given to me by God. As is recognized in words like "salvation" and "damnation," the call of destiny has a peculiar finality.

The agape of God consists in the bestowal of a destiny, and that of human beings in its recognition through faith. Since a destiny is not a matter of empirical observation, a person with a destiny is, so to speak, invisible. But every person has a destiny. Hence the process of mutual scrutiny is in vain, and even the most objective judgments of other people are fundamentally false. Agape arises from a realization of this and is therefore expressed in a refusal to judge.

The Lord of all time and existence has taken a personal interest in every human being, an interest that is compassionate and unwearying. The Christian universe is peopled exclusively with royalty. What does this mean for society?

To speak cautiously, the concept of the exalted individual implies that governments — indeed, all persons who wield power — must treat individuals with care. This can mean various things — for example, that individuals are to be fed and sheltered when they are destitute, listened to when they speak, or merely left alone so long as they do not break the law and fairly tried if they do. But however variously care may be defined, it always means that human beings are not to be treated like the things we use and discard or just leave lying about. They deserve attention. This spare standard has of course been frequently and grossly violated by people who call themselves Christians. It has not been without force, however. Even in our own secularized times people who are useless or burdensome, hopelessly ill or guilty of terrible crimes, are sometimes treated with extraordinary consideration and patience.

The modest standard of care implies other, more demanding standards. Equality is one of these; no one is to be casually sacrificed. No natural, social, or even moral differences justify exceptions to this rule. Of course destinies make people not equal but, rather, incomparable; equality is a measurement and dignity is immeasurable. But according to Christian claims, every person has been immeasurably dignified. Faith discerns no grounds for making distinctions, and the distinctions made by custom and

17

ambition are precarious before God. "Many that are first will be last, and the last first." Not only love but humility as well — the humility of not anticipating the judgments of God — impels us towards the standard of equality.

No one, then, belongs at the bottom, enslaved, irremediably poor, consigned to silence; this is equality. This points to another standard: that no one should be left outside, an alien and a barbarian. Agape implies universality. Greeks and Hebrews in ancient times were often candidly contemptuous of most of the human race. Even Jesus, although not contemptuous of Gentiles, conceived of his mission as primarily to Israel. However, Jesus no doubt saw the saving of Israel as the saving of all humankind, and his implicit universalism became explicit, and decisive for the history of the world, in the writings and missionary activity of Paul. Christian universalism (as well as Christian egalitarianism) was powerfully expressed by Paul when he wrote that "there is neither Jew nor Greek, there is neither slave nor free, there is neither male nor female; for you are all one in Christ Jesus."

Christian universalism was reinforced by the universalism of the later Stoics, who created the ideal of an all-embracing city of reason — cosmopolis. Medieval Christians couched their universalist outlook in Hellenic terms. Thus two streams of thought, from Israel and Greece, flowed together. As a result the world today, although divided among nations often ferociously self-righteous and jealous, is haunted by the vision of a global community. War and national rivalry seem unavoidable, but they burden the human conscience. Searing poverty prevails in much of the world, as it always has, but no longer is it unthinkingly accepted in either the rich nations or the poor. There is a shadowy but widespread awareness, which Christianity has had much to do with creating, that one person cannot be indifferent to the destiny of another person anywhere on earth. It is hardly too much to say that the idea of the exalted individual is the spiritual center of Western politics. Although this idea is often forgotten and betrayed, were it erased from our minds our politics would probably become altogether what it is at present only in part — an affair of expediency and self-interest.

The exalted individual is not an exclusively Christian principle. There are two ways in which, without making any religious assumptions, we may sense the infinite worth of an individual. One way is love. Through personal love, or through the sympathy by which personal love is extended (although at the same time weakened), we sense the measureless worth of a few, and are able to surmise that what we sense in a few may be present in all. In short, to love some (it is, as Dostoevsky suggested, humanly impossible to love everyone) may give rise to the idea that all are worthy of love. Further, the idea of the exalted individual may become a secular value through reason, as it did for the Stoics. Reason tells me that each person is one and not more than one. Hence my claims upon others are rightfully matched by their claims upon me. Simple fairness, which even a child can understand, is implicitly egalitarian and universal; and it is reasonable.

Can love and reason, though, undergird our politics if faith suffers a further decline? That is doubtful. Love and reason are suggestive, but they lack definite political implications. Greeks of the Periclean Age, living at the summit of the most brilliant period of Western civilization, showed little consciousness of the notion that every individual bears an indefeasible and incomparable dignity. Today why should those who assume that God is dead entertain such a notion? This question is particularly compelling in view of a human characteristic very unlike exaltation.

3

THE FALLEN INDIVIDUAL

The fallen individual is not someone other than the exalted individual. Every human being is fallen and exalted both. This paradox is familiar to all informed Christians. Yet it is continually forgotten — partly, perhaps, because it so greatly complicates the task of dealing with evil in the world, and no doubt partly because we hate to apply it to ourselves; although glad to recall our exaltation, we are reluctant to remember our fallenness. It is vital to political understanding, however, to do both. If the concept of the exalted individual defines the highest value under God, the concept of the fallen individual defines the situation in which that value must be sought and defended.

The principle that a human being is sacred yet morally degraded is hard for common sense to grasp. It is apparent to most of us that some people are morally degraded. It is ordinarily assumed, however, that other people are morally upright and that these alone possess dignity. From this point of view all is simple and logical. The human race is divided roughly between good people, who possess the infinite worth we attribute to individuals, and bad people, who do not. The basic problem of life is for the good people to gain supremacy over, and perhaps eradicate, the bad people. This view appears in varied forms: in Marxism, where the human race is divided between a world-redeeming class and a class that is exploitative and condemned; in some expressions of American nationalism, where the division — at least, until recently — has been between "the free world" and demonic communism; in Western films, where virtuous heroes kill bandits and lawless Indians.

This common model of life's meaning is drastically irreligious, because it places reliance on good human beings and not on God. It has no room for the double insight that the evil are not beyond the reach of divine mercy nor the good beyond the need for it. It is thus antithetical to Christianity, which maintains that human beings are justified by God alone, and that all are sacred and none are good.

The proposition that none are good does not mean merely that none are perfect. It means that all are persistently and deeply inclined toward evil. All are sinful. In a few sin is so effectively suppressed that it seems to have been destroyed. But this is owing to God's grace, Christian principles imply, not to human good-ness, and those in whom it has happened testify emphatically that this is so. Saints claim little credit for themselves.

Nothing in Christian doctrine so offends people today as the stress on sin. It is morbid and self-destructive, supposedly, to depreciate ourselves in this way. Yet the Christian view is not implausible. The twentieth century, not to speak of earlier ages (often assumed to be more barbaric), has displayed human evil in extravagant forms. Wars and massacres, systematic torture and internment in concentration camps, have become everyday occurrences in the decades since 1914. Even in the most civilized societies subtle forms of callousness and cruelty prevail through capitalist and bureaucratic institutions. Thus our own experience indicates that we should not casually dismiss the Christian concept of sin.

According to that concept, the inclination toward evil is primarily an inclination to exalt ourselves rather than allowing ourselves to be exalted by God. We exalt ourselves in a variety of ways: for example, by power, trying to control all the things and people around us; by greed, accumulating an inequitable portion of the material goods of the world; by self-righteousness, claiming to be wholly virtuous; and so forth. Self-exaltation is carried out sometimes by individuals, sometimes by groups. It is often referred to, in all of its various forms, as "pride."

The Christian concept of sin is not adequately described, however, merely by saying that people frequently engage in evil actions. Our predisposition toward such actions is so powerful and so unyielding that it holds us captive. As Paul said, "I do not do what I want, but I do the very thing I hate." This does not imply, of course, that I am entirely depraved. If I disapprove of my evil acts, then I am partly good. However, if I persist in evil in the face of my own disapproval, then I am not only partly evil but also incapable of destroying the evil in my nature and enthroning the good. I am, that is to say, a prisoner of evil, even if I am not wholly evil.

This imprisonment is sometimes called "original sin," not because one must take the story of Adam's disobedience literally but because it points to the mysterious truth that our captivity by evil originates in a primal and iniquitous choice on the part of every person. I persistently fail to attain goodness because I have turned away from goodness and set my face toward evil.

The political value of the doctrine of original sin lies in its recognition that our evil tendencies are not in the nature of a problem that we can rationally comprehend and deliberately solve. To say that the source of sin is sin is to say that sin is underivable and inexplicable. A sinful society is not like a malfunctioning machine, something to be checked and quickly repaired.

Sin is ironic. Its intention is self-exaltation, its result is self-debasement. In trying to ascend, we fall. The reason for this is not hard to understand. We are exalted by God; in declaring our independence from God, we cast ourselves down. In other words, sin concerns not just our actions and our nature but also the setting of our lives. By sin we cast ourselves into a degraded sphere of existence, a sphere Christians often call "the world." Human beings belong to the world through sin. They look at one another as objects; they manipulate, mutilate, and kill one another. In diverse ways, some subtle and some shocking, some relatively innocuous and some devastating, they continually depersonalize themselves and others. They behave as inhabitants of the world they have sin fully formed rather than of the earth created by God. Original sin is the quiet determination, deep in everyone, to stay inside the world. Every sinful act is a violation of the personal being that continually, in freedom, vision, and love, threatens the world. The archetype of sin is the reduction of a person to the thing we call a corpse.

4

THE MAN-GOD VERSUS
THE GOD-MAN

When the paradox of simultaneous exaltation and fallenness collapses, it is replaced by either cynicism or (to use a term that is accurate but masks the destructive character of the attitude it refers to) idealism.

Cynicism measures the value of human beings by their manifest qualities and thus esteems them very slightly. It concludes, in effect, that individuals are not exalted, because they are fallen. Idealism refuses this conclusion. It insists that the value of human beings, or of some of them, is very great. It is not so simplistic, however, as to deny the incongruity of their essential value and their manifest qualities. Rather, it asserts that this incongruity can be resolved by human beings on their own, perhaps through political revolution or psychotherapy. Human beings can exalt themselves.

We shall dwell in this discussion on idealism, partly because idealism is much more tempting and therefore much more common than cynicism. Idealism is exhilirating, whereas cynicism, as anything more than a youthful experiment, is grim and discouraging. We shall dwell on idealism also because it is so much more dangerous than it looks. The dangers of cynicism are evident; that a general contempt for human beings is apt to be socially and politically destructive scarcely needs to be argued. But idealism looks benign. It is important to understand why its appearance is misleading.

Idealism in our time is commonly a form of collective pride. Human beings exalt themselves by exalting a group. Each one of course exalts the singular and separate self in some manner. In most people, however, personal pride needs reinforcement through a common ideal or emotion, such as nationalism. Hence the rise of collective pride. To exalt ourselves, we exalt a nation, a class, or even the whole of humanity in some particular manifestations like science. Such pride is alluring. It assumes grandiose and enthralling proportions yet it seems selfless, because not one person alone but a class or nation or some other collectivity is exalted. It can be at once more extreme and less offensive than personal pride.

To represent the uncompromising and worldly character of modern idealism we may appropriately use the image of the man-god. This image is a reversal of the Christian concept of the God-man, Christ. The order of the terms obviously is crucial. In the case of the God-man, it indicates the source of Christ's divinity as understood in Christian faith. God took the initiative. To reverse the order of the terms and affirm the man-god is to say that human beings become divine on their own initiative. Here pride reaches its most extreme development. The dignity bestowed on human beings by God, in Christian faith, is now claimed as a quality that human beings can acquire through their own self-creating acts.

In using the concept of the man-god, I do not mean to suggest that divinity is explicitly attributed to certain human beings. Even propagandists, to say nothing of philosophers, are more subtle than that. What happens is simply that qualities traditionally attributed to God are shifted to a human group or type. The qualities thus assigned are various — perfect understanding, perhaps, or unfailing fairness. Illustrative are the views of three great intellectual figures, familiar to everyone, yet so diversely interpreted that the fundamental character of their thought — and their deep similarity — is sometimes forgotten.

Friedrich Nietzsche set forth the ideal of the man-god more literally and dramatically than any other writer. Nietzsche's thinking was grounded in a bitter repudiation of Christianity, and he devoted much of his life to scouring human consciousness in order to cleanse it of every Christian idea and emotion. In this way his philosophy became a comprehensive critique of Western civilization, as well as a foreshadowing of an alternative civilization. It is, as practically everyone now recognizes, remarkable in its range, subtlety, and complexity; Nietzsche is not easily classified or epitomized. It can nevertheless be argued that the dramatic center of his lifework lay in the effort to overthrow the standard of Christian love and to wipe out the idea that every human being deserves respect — leading Nietzsche to attack such norms in the field of politics as equality and democracy. If Christian faith is spurned, Nietzsche held, with the courage that was one of the sources of his philosophical greatness, then Christian morality must also be spurned. Agape has no rightful claim on our allegiance. And not only does agape lack all moral authority but it has a destructive effect on society and culture. It inhibits the rise of superior human beings to the heights of glory, which we realize at last, are not inhabited by God. By exalting the common person, who is entirely lacking in visible distinction and glory, agape subverts the true order of civilization. The divine quality that Nietzsche claimed for humanity was power — the power not only of great political leaders like Julius Caesar and Napoleon but also of philosophers, writers, and artists, who impose intricate and original forms of order on chaotic material. Such power, in the nature of things, can belong only to a few. These few are human gods. Their intrinsic splendor overcomes the absurdity that erupted with the death of the Christian God, and justifies human existence.

Karl Marx is perhaps not only as well known among Christian intellectuals as even the most celebrated theologians but also as influential. The familiar saying "We are all Marxists now" dramatizes the fact that Marx's views on such matters as class and capitalism are part of the furniture of the modern mind. Christian writers are not exceptions; spontaneously they think in some measure in Marxist terms. A considerable number of them can even be called Marxist Christians — an appellation fully justified in the case of most liberation theologians. Marx has in that sense become a familiar member of the Christian household. When he is thus domesticated, however, we tend to forget what he really thought. We may forget that he was as apocalyptically secular and humanistic as Nietzcshe, even though he disdained the kind of elevated and poetic rhetoric that abounds in Nietzsche's writings. He called for the entire transformation of human life by human beings, and this, in Marx's mind, included the transformation of nature. The universe was to become radically — in its roots, in its sources and standards — human. True, like the Christians he scorned, and unlike Nietzsche, Marx was egalitarian. The transformation of humanity and being was envisioned as the work of multitudes, the proletariat, and not of exceptional individuals, and ahead lay justice and community rather than glorious solitude, as in Nietzsche. Nevertheless, Marx tacitly claimed for the proletariat qualities much like those attributed in the Old Testament to God — omniscience, righteousness, and historical sovereignty, all devoted to avenging past wrongs and transfiguring human existence.

Sigmund Freud, of course, avoided both the rhetoric of redemption and the thought; he regarded any great change in the character of human beings or the conditions of human life as unlikely, and by intention was a scientist, not a prophet or a revolutionary. He belongs among the heralds of the man-god, however, because of the conviction that underlay all his psychological investigations. Disorders of the soul, which for Christians derive in one way or another from sin, and hence in their ultimate origins are mysterious, Freud believed to be scientifically explicable. From this conviction it followed that the healing work Christians believe to be dependent on divine grace Freud could assign altogether to human therapy. The soul was thus severed from God (for Freud, a childish illusion) and placed in the province of human understanding and action. Not that psychoanalysis and Christianity are in all ways mutually exclusive; the many Christians who have learned from Freud testify to the contrary. But for Freud and his major followers, psychoanalysis is a comprehensive faith, not merely a set of useful hypotheses and techniques. As a faith, it attributes to humanity alone powers and responsibilities that Christians regard as divine. Human beings are exalted by virtue of purely human faculties. Freud's attitude of resignation was a matter mainly of temperament; his methods, theories, and basic assumptions have reinforced the efforts of human beings to seize the universal sovereignty that Christians assign exclusively to God.

29

Nietzsche, Marx, and Freud represent a movement by no means restricted to those who consciously follow any one of them or even to those familiar with their writings. Not only are we "all Marxists now"; it could be said with nearly equal justification that we are all Nietzscheans and Freudians. Most of us have come to assume that we ourselves are the authors of human destiny. The term "man-god" may seem extreme, but I believe that our situation is extreme. Christianity poses sweeping alternatives — destiny and fate, redemption and eternal loss, the Kingdom of God and the void of Hell. From centuries of Christian culture and education we have come habitually to think of life as structured by such extremes. Hence Christian faith may fade, but we still want to live a destiny rather than a mere life, to transform the conditions of human existence and not merely to effect improvements, to establish a perfect community and not simply a better society. Losing faith in the God-man, we inevitably begin to dream of the man-god, even though we often think of the object of our new faith as something impersonal and innocuous, like science, thus concealing from ourselves the radical nature of our dreams.

5

POLITICAL IDOLATRY

The political repercussions are profound. Most important is that all logical grounds for attributing an ultimate and immeasurable dignity to every person, regardless of outward character, disappear. Some people may gain dignity from their achievements in art, literature, or politics, but the notion that all people without exception — the most base, the most destructive, the most repellent — have equal claims on our respect becomes as absurd as would be the claim that all automobiles or all horses are of equal excellence. The standard of agape collapses. It becomes explicable only on Niezsche's terms: as a device by which the weak and failing exact from the strong and distinguished a deference they do not deserve. Thus the spiritual center of Western politics fades and vanishes. If the principle of personal dignity disappears, the kind of political order we are used to — one structured by standards such as liberty for all human beings and equality under the law — becomes indefensible.

Niezsche's stature is owing to the courage and profundity that enabled him to make this all unmistakably clear. He delineated with overpowering eloquence the consequences of giving up

Christianity, and every like view of the universe and humanity. His approval of those consequences and his hatred of Christianity give force to his argument. Many would like to think that there are no consequences — that we can continue treasuring the life and welfare, the civil rights and political authority, of every person without believing in a God who renders such attitudes and conduct compelling. Niezsche shows that we cannot. We cannot give up the Christian God — and the transcendence given other names in other faiths — and go on as before. We must give up Christian morality too. If the God-man is nothing more than an illusion, the same thing is true of the idea that every individual possesses incalculable worth.

It is true, as we have seen, that love and reason provide intimations of such worth — but intimations alone; they provide little basis for overruling the conclusions of our senses. The denial of the God-man and of God's merciful love of sinful humanity is a denial of destiny, and without destiny there is simply life. But life calls forth respect only in proportion to its intensity and quality. Except in the case of infants and children, we ordinarily look on those lacking in purposeful vitality with pity and disgust. Respect we spontaneously reserve for the strong and creative. If it is life we prize, then institutions that protect and care for people whose lives are faltering are worse than senseless. It is hard to think of anyone else, with the single exception of Dostoevsky, who has understood all of this as profoundly as did Niezsche.

Marx certainly did not. His mind was on matters of a different kind, matters less philosophical. The result was an illogical humanitarianism. Marx was incensed by the squalor in which the common people of his time were forced to live and by the harsh conditions and endless hours of their work. Marx sympathized deeply with the downtrodden and disinherited. But this expressed his personal qualities, not his philosophy or faith. His philosophy was a materialism that can be interpreted in differing ways but that implied, at the very least, that reality was not created by and is not governed by God; his faith was in science and human will. He provided no philosophical or religious grounds whatever for the idea that every person must be treated with care. In spite of Marx's humanitarianism, therefore, there is a link between Marxist thought and the despotic regimes that have ruled in his name. It is perfectly true, as his defenders aver, that Marx adhered to political principles quite unlike those manifest in the purges and prison camps of the Soviet Union. That such practices should claim the authority of his name is thus outrageous in a sense. Nonetheless, the connection between Marx himself and modern Marxist despots is not entirely accidental. They share the principle that a single individual does not necessarily matter.

If the denial of the God-man has destructive logical implications, it also has dangerous emotional consequences. Dostoevsky wrote that a person "cannot live without worshipping something." Anyone who denies God must worship an idol — which is not necessarily a wooden or metal figure. In our time we have seen ideologies, groups, and leaders receive divine honors. People proud of their critical and discerning spirit have rejected Christ and bowed down before Hitler, Stalin, Mao, or some other secular savior.

When disrespect for individuals is combined with political idolatry, the results can be atrocious. Both the logical and the emotional foundations of political decency are destroyed. Equality becomes nonsensical and breaks down under attack from one or another human god. Consider Lenin: as a Marxist, and like Marx an exponent of equality, under the pressures of revolution he denied equality in principle — except as an ultimate goal — and so systematically nullified it in practice as to become the founder of modern totalitarianism. When equality falls, universality is likely also to fall. Nationalism or some other form of collective pride becomes virulent, and war unrestrained. Liberty, too, is likely to vanish; it becomes a heavy personal and social burden when no God justifies and sanctifies the individual in spite of all personal deficiencies and failures.

The idealism of the man-god does not, of course, bring as an immediate and obvious consequence a collapse into unrestrained nihilism. We all know many people who do not believe in God and yet are decent and admirable. Western societies, as highly secularized as they are, retain many humane features. Not even tacitly has our sole governing maxim become the one Dostoevsky thought was bound to follow the denial of the God-man: "Everything is permitted."

This may be, however, because customs and habits formed during Christian ages keep people from professing and acting on such a maxim even though it would be logical for them to do so. If that is the case, our position is precarious, for good customs and habits need spiritual grounds, and if those are lacking, they will gradually, or perhaps suddenly in some crisis, crumble.

To what extent are we now living on moral savings accumulated over many centuries but no longer being replenished? To what extent are those savings already severely depleted? Again and again we are told by advertisers, counselors, and other purveyors of popular wisdom that we have a right to buy the things we want and to live as we please. We should be prudent and farsighted, perhaps (although even those modest virtues are not greatly emphasized), but we are subject ultimately to no standard but self-interest. If nihilism is most obvious in the lives of wanton destroyers like Hitler, it is nevertheless present also in the lives of people who live purely as pleasure and convenience dictate.

And aside from intentions, there is a question concerning consequences. Even idealists whose good intentions for the human race are pure and strong are still vulnerable to fate because of the pride that causes them to act ambitiously and recklessly in history. Initiating chains of unforeseen and destructive consequences, they are often overwhelmed by results drastically at variance with their humane intentions. Modern revolutionaries have willed liberty and equality for everyone, not the terror and despotism they have actually created. Social reformers in the United States were never aiming at the great federal bureaucracy or at the pervasive dedication to entertainment and pleasure that characterizes the welfare state they brought into existence. There must always be a gap between intentions and results, but for those who forget that they are finite and morally flawed the gap may become a chasm. Not only Christians but almost everyone today feels the fear that we live under the sway of forces that we have set in motion — perhaps in the very process of industrialization, perhaps only at certain stages of that process, as in the creation of nuclear power — and that threaten our lives and are beyond our control.

There is much room for argument about these matters. But there is no greater error in the modern mind than the assumption that the God-man can be repudiated with impunity. The man-god may take his place and become the author of deeds wholly unintended and the victim of terrors starkly in contrast with the benign intentions lying at their source. The irony of sin is in this way reproduced in the irony of idealism: exalting human beings in their supposed virtues and powers, idealism undermines them. Exciting fervent expectations, it leads toward despair.

6

IDEOLOGY AND AMBIGUITY

Practically everyone today agrees that "being good," in a
political sense, depends on recognizing the measureless
worth of the human being. When this recognition
is translated into ideological terms, such as liberalism and
conservatism, however, agreement vanishes. The main
moral assumption underlying the discussion above becomes
controversial. Nevertheless, we have to ask what the ideological
implications of Christianity are, for this is simply to inquire about
the practical meaning of the ideas that we have been discussing
and thus to carry the argument to its logical conclusion.

In asking about ideology, however, we immediately encounter
something that seemingly undermines any ideological commitment. This is an implicit political ambiguity. This ambiguity is
deeply rooted in Christian principles, and must at the outset be
taken into account.

In the Christian view, while every individual is exalted, society is not. On the contrary, every society is placed in question,
for a society is a mere worldly order and a mere human creation
and can never do justice to the glory of the human beings within

it. The exaltation of the individual reveals the baseness of society. It follows that our political obligations are indeterminate and equivocal. If we recognize what God has done — so Christian principles imply — we shall be limitlessly respectful of human beings but wary of society. Yet human beings live in society, and we meet them there or not at all. Hence we cannot stand wholly apart from society without failing in our responsibilities to the human beings whom God has exalted. So far as we are responsive to God, we must live within human kingdoms as creatures destined to be fellow citizens in God's Kingdom. This obligation gives rise to a political stance that is ambiguous and, in a world of devastatingly unambiguous ideologies, unique: humane and engaged, but also hesitant and critical.

Christianity implies skepticism concerning political ideals and plans. For Christianity to be wedded indissolubly to any of them (as it often has been, "Christian socialism" and Christian celebrations of "the spirit of democratic capitalism" being examples) is idolatrous and thus subversive of Christian faith.

Trying to take into account both the profound evil in human nature and the immense hope in the human situation, as Christians must, leads inevitably to what reformers and radicals — particularly those of the Third World, surrounded as they are by impoverished multitudes — are apt to regard as fatal equivocations. It leads, as I have already indicated, to a critical spirit and to qualified commitments. It would be easy to charge that such a posture reflects the self-interest and complacency of those who do not suffer from the injustice characterizing existing structures. Equivocation, it may be said, is one of the luxuries of bourgeois life in the industrial world.

Still, a Christian in the United States, without being particularly discerning or morally sensitive, can see at least two things not so clearly visible to Third World Christian writers, particularly those liberation theologians who long for immediate social transformation. One of these is the universal disaster of revolution. There is perhaps not a single example in our time of a determined effort to produce swift and sweeping change which has not ended in tyranny; such efforts have often also ended in abominations, such as those witnessed in recent times in Cambodia, incalculably worse than those perpetrated by the old social order.

The second thing a Christian in a prosperous industrial nation can see is visible because it is near at hand: that life can be culturally vulgar, morally degraded, and spiritually vacuous even under conditions of substantial justice. Not that justice has been fully achieved in the United States. But it has been approximated closely enough for us to begin to gauge its significance. We can begin to see that justice does not necessarily mean an entirely good society. The great masses of people in the United States enjoy historically unprecedented prosperity, in stark contrast with conditions in the Third World. Accompanying this prosperity, however, are signs — too numerous and flagrant to need mentioning — of moral cynicism, spiritual frivolity, and despair. If revolutions make plain the power of sin — its ability to captivate idealistic reformers — mass society displays the ingenuity of sin. Human beings in their passion for justice have not devised institutions that they cannot in their pride and selfishness outwit.

It may seem that the ideological meaning of Christianity is becoming clear: Christianity is solidly, if covertly, on the side of the status quo. It is conservative. There are good reasons for arguing, however, that Christianity cannot logically be conservative but is rather — in its own distinctive fashion — radical.

7

A HESITANT RADICALISM

The Christian record in the annals of reform, it must be granted, is not impressive. Christians have accepted, and sometimes actively supported, slavery, poverty, and almost every other common social evil. They have often condemned such evils in principle but failed to oppose them in practice. Faith does not necessarily conquer selfishness and is particularly unlikely to do so when connected with an established religion and thus with privileged groups. That Christianity has in various times and places, and in various ways, been an established religion is perhaps the major reason why it has been implicated in injustices such as slavery, serfdom, and the oppressive wage labor of early capitalism.

Nevertheless, Christianity in essence is not conservative. The notion that it is (the historical record aside) probably stems mainly from the fact that Christians share with conservatives a consciousness of the fallibility of human beings. The two camps occupy common anthropological ground. But the consciousness of human fallibility is far keener among Christians than among conservatives, for Christians are skeptical of human arrangements that typically command deep respect in conservatives. Thus, Christians cannot logically assume that the antiquity of institutions provides any assurance of their justice or efficacy. They realize, if they consult Christian principles, that long-standing customs and traditions embody not only the wisdom of generations but also the wickedness — in particular, the determination of dominant groups to preserve their powers and privileges.

Christians are also mistrustful of aristocracies and elites. Conservatives typically commend the rule of long-ascendant minorities, those certified by the established order as wise and noble. But Paul, addressing early Christians in Corinth, noted that "not many of you were wise according to worldly standards, not many were powerful, not many were of noble birth." New Testament passages indicate that Christ had a special concern for the despised and disinherited, the ignorant and unsophisticated. "God chose what is foolish in the world to shame the wise." The attitude expressed in such a passage is remote from the typical conservative reverence for minorities of inherited rank and traditional learning.

Conservatives (like non-Christian radicals) commonly assume that sin can be circumvented by human skill. In the conservative view, allowing only those institutional changes that are gradual and protracted, and according authority to traditional elites, will accomplish this. For Christians, sin is circumvented only by grace. It is certainly not circumvented by society, the form that sinful men and women give to the fallen world.

In America conservatives believe that sin is effectively redirected to the common good through the market. The alchemy of capitalist competition transmutes sin into virtue. But it is difficult to see how any Christian who fully grasps Christian principles can be an unqualified supporter of capitalism. Insofar as the market governs social relations, people are forced into acquisitive rivalry;

to count in any way on a gift of "daily bread" rather than on money in the bank would be the mark of a fool. Acquisitive success is candidly equated with virtue and personal worth naively measured in material terms. Charity is often bestowed on the needy, but it is a matter of personal generosity, not of justice or community; and it is unsanctioned in capitalist theory. No principles could be more thoroughly anticommunal than those of capitalism. Indeed, capitalism is probably more anticommunal in theory than in practice, for human beings cannot be as consistently selfish and calculating as capitalist doctrine calls on them to be. Capitalism has one bond with Christianity — the premise that human beings are ordinarily selfish. A system that enables an industrial society to achieve a degree of order and efficiency without depending on either human goodness or governmental coercion cannot be entirely despised. Nevertheless, even if capitalism worked as well as its supporters claim, it would by Christian standards fail morally and spiritually.

But if Christians are more pessimistic about human beings and about social devices like the market than are conservatives, how can they act on the side of serious social change? How can they do anything but cling to all institutions, however unjust, that counteract the chaotic potentialities of human beings and achieve some sort of order? There are three answers to these questions.

First of all, Christian ideas place one in a radical — that is, critical and adverse — relationship to established institutions. The Kingdom of God is a judgment on existing society, and a symbol of its impermanence. Jesus was crucified because his presence and preaching were profoundly unsettling to reigning religious and political groups. Jesus did not seek the violent

43

overthrow of these groups, but neither did he show much concern for their stability.

Further, these attitudes have to be acted on. This is a matter of spiritual integrity. To anticipate the coming of the Kingdom of God is merely sentimental, a private frivolity, unless one tries to reshape society according to the form of the imminent community, a form defined by equality and universality and requiring particular attention to the disinherited and oppressed.

Finally, however, to take it for granted that all attempted reforms will fail would be as presumptuous as to assume that they will succeed. It is not only sinful human beings who are at work in history, Christians believe, but God as well. Agape is not merely a standard of personal conduct, powerless over events. In exalting individuals, it discloses the inner meaning of history. To practice love is to be allied with the deepest currents of life. From a Christian standpoint, a frightened refusal of all social change would be highly inappropriate.

Clearly the immediate political aims of Christians are not necessarily different from those of secular radicals and reformers. Their underlying attitudes are different, however. The Christian sense of the depth and stubbornness of evil in human beings, along with the faith that the universe under the impetus of grace is moving toward radical re-creation, gives a distinctive cast to the Christian conception of political action and social progress.

Secular conceptions of reform are apt to be characterized by optimistic oversimplifications and distortions. American reformers, for example, typically assume that human beings are both reasonable and just and that beneficent social change is therefore easy. The main thing necessary, after identifying a problem, is to devise and propagate a rational solution. Poverty, crime, class conflict, war, and all other great social evils can gradually but surely be eliminated. Good will and intelligence, well organized and fully informed (through the studies of social scientists), will suffice. Such illusions stem from a dilemma noted above. It is difficult for secular reformers to reconcile their sense of the dignity of individuals with a recognition of the selfishness and perversity of individuals. They are thus led persistently to exaggerate human goodness. Trying to match their view of human nature with their belief in human dignity, they fail to see how human beings actually behave or to understand the difficulties and complexities of reform.

Tocqueville suggested approvingly that Christianity tends to make a people "circumspect and undecided," with "its impulses...checked and its works unfinished." This expresses well the spirit of reform inherent in Christian faith. Christianity is radical, but it is also hesitant. This is partly, of course, because Christianity restrains our self-assurance. Efforts at social transformation must always encounter unforeseen complexities, difficulties, limits, and tragedies. Caution is in order. But Christian hesitancy has deeper grounds than prudence and more compelling motives than wariness of practical blunders. Hesitation expresses a consciousness of the mystery of being and the dignity of every person. It provides a moment for consulting destiny. Recent decades have seen heroic political commitments in behalf of social reform, but hesitation has been evident mainly in the service of self-interest. Christian faith, however, suggests that hesitation should have a part in our most conscientious deeds. It is a formality that is fitting when we cross the frontier between meditation and action. And like all significant formalities, it is a mark of respect — for God and for the creatures with whom we share the earth.

Some will dislike the implication that "being good" consists in being radical; others will think it strange to link radicalism with hesitation or religious faith. I suggest, however, that the main task facing political goodness in our time is that of maintaining responsible hope. Responsible hope is hesitant because it is cognizant of the discouraging actualities of collective life; it is radical because it measures those actualities against the highest standards of imagination and faith. Whether so paradoxical a stance can be sustained without transcendental connections — without God — is doubtful.

We live in a disheartening century — "the worst so far," as someone has said. There have never before been wars so destructive as the series of conflicts that erupted in 1914; never have tyrannies been so frenzied and all-consuming as those established by Nazism and communism. All great political causes have failed. Socialism has eventuated in the rule either of privileged ideological bureaucrats or of comfortable, listless masses; liberal reform in America has at least for a time passed away, leaving stubborn injustices and widespread cynicism; conservatism has come to stand for an illogical combination of market economics and truculent nationalism. Most of the human race lives in crushing poverty, and the privileged minority in societies where industrial abundance undergirds a preoccupation with material comfort and an atmosphere of spiritual inanity.

It is not just that hope itself is difficult to maintain in our situation. One is forced, so to speak, to hope alone. After all that has happened, in what party or cause or movement can one find a hope that can be unreservedly shared? Inherent in the disheartenment of our century is the impossibility of believing any longer in political commitment. And to draw back from commitment is to face political solitude. The individual must find a way of standing

46

for authentic values with little or no human support. A radicalism that is hesitant must also be solitary.

If the great causes and movements all have failed, and unqualified political commitments have become impossible, why not, as Paul asked, eat and drink, since tomorrow we die? This is a question that secular reason should take far more seriously than it ever has.

It is a question to which all of us need an answer. The need is partly political. There can be no decent polities unless many people can resist the historical discouragement so natural in our times. The consumer society and fascism exemplify the possible outcome when nations are populated predominantly by people incapable of the hesitation in which reality needs to be faced or the hope in which it must be judged and reshaped.

The need is also personal. In its depths the life of an individual is historical and political because it is one with the lives of all human beings. To despair of history is to despair of one's own humanity. Today we are strongly tempted to split the individual and history, the personal and the political. When this occurs, personal being is truncated and impoverished. People in earlier times of bewilderment and disillusionment, such as the era of the downfall of the ancient city-state system, were similarly tempted, and a standard of life first clearly enunciated by Epicurus in the aftermath of the Macedonian conquest of the city-states is still, in the twentieth century, attractive. Epicurus called for withdrawal from public life and political activity; he argued that everything essential to one's humanity, such as friendship, can be found in the private sphere. Personal life thus is salvaged from the raging torrent of history. But it is also mutilated, for it is severed from the human situation in its global scope and its political contours.

47

The absorption of Americans in the pleasures of buying and consuming, of mass entertainment and sports, suggests an Epicurean response to our historical trials. The dangers — erosion of the grounds of political health and impairment of personal being — are evident.

Being good politically means not only valuing the things that are truly valuable but also having the strength to defend those things when they are everywhere being attacked and abandoned. Such strength is exemplified by Dietrich Bonhoeffer, the great German pastor and theologian, who uncompromisingly opposed the Nazi regime from the beginning, even to the extent of returning to Germany from a guaranteed haven in America to join the anti-Hitler resistance. Arrested by the Gestapo, he was killed at the end of the war. One of Bonhoeffer's prayers, composed in prison, was, "Give me the hope that will deliver me from fear and faintheartedness." Much that I have tried to say in the preceding pages might be summarized simply in this question: If we turn away from transcendence, from God, what will deliver us from a politically fatal fear and faintheartedness?

CPSIA information can be obtained at www.ICGtesting.com
Printed in the USA
BVOW06s1157201016

465449BV00008B/125/P